THE REDEEMED HEART

THE REDEEMED HEART

LATRICE J. SIMMONS

ISBN: 979-8-2181422-4-7

I dedicate this book to anyone who feels lost after battling any heartache, hurt, or betrayal. Know that God sees you and will provide healing in the most beautiful and unexpected ways.

CONTENTS

REVIEWS FOR *THE REDEEMED HEART*

"Latrice describes *The Redeemed Heart* as "spiritual open heart surgery" and her book truly delivers on this concept! Like a skilled surgeon, she carefully and effectively opens your heart with her words to reveal the good, the bad, and the ugly. She gives you tools to work through hurts and helps you reach restoration with Jesus Christ. Her message can show you how to face your issues and emerge from the dark places into the light. You can live the life God has intended for you—free from the pain of the past and moving forward into the beautiful future."

-Alexis A. Goring, author and owner of Writer at Heart Editorial Services

"Reading this made me feel like I was listening to a friend, but also as if God was speaking directly to me about me. Anyone who has ever been hurt or has a hard time forgiving will benefit from reading this book."

-Amber N. Robinson, executive pastor, City of Hope-Columbia

"Thought-provoking, realistic, and personal. This book is good for any believer of Christ who may be seeking help and understanding of their feelings but also who are seeking help in how to build with God."

-Tequila Pauling, prophetess and life coach

"The solace it gave me, felt like a breath of fresh air, after holding my breath for so long and exhaling. Each word was selected carefully and I felt the conviction of each one. Just from the introduction I felt like I was literally reading my healing and creating an altar. This made me ready to lay at God's hem and ask Him to heal me. Latrice has created and commanded a space for her audience. She is definitely redeeming hearts, just as its been titled."

-Tonisha Conyers, wife, mother, and mentor

Redeemed [ri-deemd]

adjective

1. *Theology.* (in Christianity) having been saved or delivered from sin or its consequences

2. having been paid, recovered, bought back, or exchanged for money or other goods

3. having been discharged or fulfilled

4. having made amends for or overcome some wrongdoing or fault

THE HEART NEEDS REDEMPTION

The word "heart" is mentioned over 800 times in the Bible. If God chooses to use this word so often, there must be some relevance and importance. What is it about the heart? Why does God repeatedly bring it to our attention? Spiritually, the heart is the home of our character and emotions. Physically, it is the source from which all blood pumps and flows. Our physical heart feeds blood throughout our bodies. Similarly, our spiritual heart does the same, feeding our emotions into our thoughts and actions.

God wants to touch the deepest parts of our hearts. The parts so secretive we keep hidden from those closest to us. The things that we suffer with but are too ashamed to say aloud. Those issues that we can't even admit to ourselves. They are some of the ugliest parts we try to keep at bay or ignore. Shame keeps us bound and silences us until we become incapable of being honest about our struggles.

There are leaks in the hearts of so many people who may not even realize it. Leaks happen slowly. But over time, when left undiagnosed and untreated, it leaves an irreversible mess. Even after it's healed and restored, a residue remains of bad choices and negative encounters. So now, others are forced to live in the hurt and trauma we have placed on them that comes from our brokenness. We create cycles of heart wounds. These wounds spill over into how we interact with people and treat ourselves. The purpose of this book is to challenge the insecurities that lie in your heart and deceive your mind. Many of us have become so comfortable living out of our wounds that God cannot elevate us in the way He desires. My prayer for you as you read this message is to know that you are seen. You are not alone, and there is redemption for the brokenhearted.

Before you read the first chapter, please note these few reminders about how this book is structured: Each chapter ends with a short summary titled "The Heart of the Issue". This is the underlying core of the heart problem that will explain how it leads us astray. Use this as a way to reflect on your own heart's emotions and behaviors. Ponder how you've progressed or imagine where you would like to see improvement. After you have reflected, the section titled "Invocation" is an opportunity to pray about different issues plaguing your heart. It is an invitation to God, requesting His assistance, presence, and authority to guide you through this spiritual open heart surgery as you read this book.

The world and sometimes even the Church, have wrongly shown us how to heal. We need God and we also have to be honest about the hurts that plague us. By the time you reach the end of this book, you will be more acquainted with your heart and its desires. You will also learn how to discern the heart of God concerning you and your life. Let my personal stories be a testament that inner redemption is a process. Choosing to heal your heart is not quick nor painless work. But I've learned that when God redeems your heart, He also redeems your time and your hurts by giving it a new meaning and new narrative. Doesn't that sound refreshing? It's time to reclaim your redemption story. And that journey begins now.

"As water reflects the face, so one's life reflects the heart."

- Proverbs 27:19

CHAPTER 1

LOOKING INTO THE MIRROR

How do you see yourself? Do you take the time to evaluate how you see yourself and how that affects the way you present yourself to the world? How you see yourself determines how you interact with others and yourself. Self-perception is the key to how we choose to show up in the world—whether it's confident or insecure, humble or arrogant, fearful or courageous. How you feel about yourself matters.

When you see yourself as engaging and beautiful, you are more likely to communicate your confidence when interacting with others. In the same way, if you see yourself as worthless and boring, you are likely to communicate your insecurity to others by way of passivity or shyness. And being a reserved person isn't wrong or sinful. Some of us are naturally quieter than others (myself included). But the truth is, many of us have claimed to be introverted to hide behind our shyness because we see ourselves as unworthy and believe others will perceive us the same way. The same is true about trust.

Trust requires awareness and belief in the ability of yourself or others to achieve or overcome something. Lacking confidence in your abilities and character causes you to look outward with distrust and unbelief, making you shrink under hardships and pressure. If you believe you are untrustworthy, you probably generally see others as untrustworthy. Now that we have a better understanding of self-perception, what does it have to do with the heart? And how does it translate into our relationship with God?

Learn to Deal with You

For most of my life, I was convinced that I was less than an ordinary person, destined to live a quiet and invisible life. And that feeling didn't change much after I started my journey with Christ. I didn't wake up instantly healed from low self-esteem the next day. Honestly, it wasn't a concern of mine. In the past, I was okay with playing small because in my heart, I believed I was small and could make no impact in the world. God had to start an inner work within me before I even considered changing my self-perception.

He began to revive dead dreams and desires in my heart. He showed me visions of my future and that's when the inner tension started to build because what I saw in myself and how God saw me were contradictory. I spent a lot of time ignoring and arguing the things God said about me, even when He would confirm it repeatedly.

My heart wasn't ready to receive it. It doesn't matter how much we pray for a thing to come to pass. If our hearts aren't open to receiving that dream then we will never be able to hold our blessings. And if we never believe we are worthy to achieve amazing things, we become a walking prophecy of that belief.

The cycle of low self-esteem is ironic because the attempt to hide leaves you alone with the one person you try to outrun the most: yourself. Some of us walk around hating ourselves. We don't acknowledge it because we don't know how to put words to it. Instead of expressing our fears and shame, we walk around in clothes of anger, isolation, and lowliness. You extend grace to others, yet when it comes to yourself you can't be bothered to show self-care and compassion. Some of us were never taught how to love ourselves because those who raised us didn't have the right understanding or tools to do it. This is okay, but now is the time to unlearn bad habits and embrace new ones that better serve you.

Your Eden Story

When did you start having a negative self-perception? When did your identity begin to shift from who God says you are to who the enemy, your family, friends, or the world says you are? Our experiences may look different from each other but our roots are the same. It all starts with sin. The Bible informs us of how our perception as humans was altered. If you're not familiar with the story of creation, here's a recap: God created this world and filled the Earth with all sorts of living creations like the fish in the sea, the birds in the air and the animals on the land. He crowned His creation with the very first humans to ever exist: Adam and Eve.

God gave dominion and authority to humans to build using natural resources from the earth, to multiply by birthing more humans, and cultivate the land. We were designed to live in perfect harmony and intimate fellowship with God in the Garden of Eden. Adam and Eve spent time with God face-to-face before they were deceived by the devil and made a choice that stripped humans of the ability to be that close to God in that way. Satan (the devil) interrupted the human relationship with God by twisting God's instructions about not eating the fruit from the tree of the knowledge of good and evil. Read the Bible book of Genesis, chapter three, for details. Long story short: The enemy's deception led to Adam and Eve disobeying and doubting God's word. They chose to eat the forbidden fruit. This sin awakened them to a reality they should have never known. Now we live in the result of their initial sin, waiting for Jesus Christ to return so we can be in perfect harmony and fellowship face-to-face with God again.

We all have an Eden story. It represents the origin of when we, just like Adam and Eve after they sinned, started hiding from the God who created us. This shame was introduced by an outside force that told you about the worst parts of yourself before you let God define you. God's plan never was for you to walk in shame, believing you're not good enough to serve Him or accomplish your dreams. He has always seen you as beloved, beautiful, and redeemed. His desire, ever since your Eden story, has been to restore your perception of yourself, and for you to be reconciled with Him.

The Heart of the Issue:

If we only rely on how we see ourselves and what we think others see about us, we have made an idol of ourselves and people. How much longer are you willing to allow external noise to steal your God-given identity and inheritance? If how we think and behave are rooted outside of God, we have to evaluate what or who we have made greater than Him. Only an artist can give the true interpretation of their work, and as the Chief Artist, God is the only one who can truly define His creation. Your journey will become more fulfilling when you are transparent and your heart is open to the truth.

Invocation:

Lord, I repent for seeing myself as less than who You created me to be. Help my heart to accept the inheritance You willingly gave to me. Help me to believe that Jesus vindicated my shame on the cross. I can now walk in radiance knowing I have always been chosen and redeemed, according to Your will. In Jesus's name I pray. Amen.

"A heart at peace gives life to the body, but envy rots the bones."

-Proverbs 14:30

CHAPTER 2

THE COMPARISON TRAP

"You see the best in others, but can't see the best in yourself."

People have told me that phrase countless times in my life. It's a gift I have. I can see the best characteristics and potential in other people and encourage them to see beyond their flaws, but I fall short of doing that for myself. The comparison trap thrives within those conditions. Seeing the best in everyone but yourself can lead to a cycle of comparing someone else's talents and attributes to your own. The way comparison manifests in your life and mine may look different but the end result is the same: detriment to our mental and spiritual health.

The Truth about Me vs. Comparison

The spirit of comparison does not always appear in the form of jealousy and harbored resentment towards others. I've learned that comparison is double-sided because either we use our lives to measure others or we use the lives of others to measure our own life. Both ways are equally incorrect. The first way results in pride and thinking better of yourself. The latter results in shame and self-condemnation, thinking less of yourself. Shame is a mark I am familiar with and have long wished was removed from my story. It's a feeling that's hard to live with and sometimes even harder to describe. The best way I can describe it is there is a voice in my head that sounds like me, retelling every mistake I have ever made.

This voice says I should be embarrassed and ashamed of what I've done. This same voice controls what I say and do during important and mundane moments: in meetings, while I'm leading in church, going to the store, attending social gatherings or interacting with people in any setting, recording a video, and releasing my content into the world. That voice of shame then evolves into a comparison monster that seeks to undermine any work and progress I've made.

Social media has made this comparison monster even more prevalent in my life. Platform building can easily become a doorway to comparison for the enemy to exploit. Followers, views, comments, likes, and shares become our measurement tools for our impact and effectiveness. When we see other people in our field exceeding the numbers we produce, we can become addicted to trying to outdo others and viewing platform viewership as a judgment of our worth. That's how comparison works. It tells you to go on Instagram and take note of every female influencer, check her number of followers then scroll through every picture of her seemingly perfect life. The voice of comparison will tell you to look up a classmate or a former friend's page who you no longer follow, just so you can see if they are "better off" after you've unfollowed them. I have done all those things, more times than I would like to admit. I have used the lives of others as a measure for my life since childhood.

As a child I compared outward appearances and characteristics a lot more. Back then, it was "She's prettier" or "She's skinnier and more athletic". Adulthood is a bit different. Now it's "She has more followers than me", "She has more influence than me", "She's more purposed than me", or "That's why she's there and I'm here". Comparison tells me that anyone who has more followers on social media or more accomplishments than me is better than me. The voice leads me to believe I should feel guilt and remorse for not having the same amount of followers and accomplishments. Or that I have done something wrong because what I have doesn't match to what the other person has. This voice of shame and comparison forces wrongdoing even when there is none.

You and I vs. Comparison

Many of us have adopted envy and comparison habits that stem from personal experiences of abandonment and rejection. Circumstances have trained our hearts and minds to believe that there is no space for our desires and gifts. Roots of rejection can cause you to see and accept the best in others while denying the opportunity to do the same for yourself. Have you ever asked yourself why you envy your friend who got married or started a family before you? Or why you are jealous of your friend who bought the house or car you always wanted? Maybe they just launched a successful business and are confidently walking in their purpose. All of this produces uneasiness and bitterness in your gut. You may appear genuinely happy for them on the surface, but there's something in you that can't seem to fully rejoice with them.

It's not because you don't believe they deserve their wins, but it's because their wins are offending the deep-seated trauma within you. You have difficulty celebrating with people because of how you view yourself. You fail relationally when you haven't mastered your relationship with God and yourself. You can serve God well outwardly. You love and care for others outwardly but inwardly may despise them. Why? Because you believe God is holding back from you, He has forgotten about you and is leaving you behind. Your life has been one fight after another fight. Fall after fall, you believe there is no way that any good can come to you. You don't believe God loves you enough to bless you with your desires. And out of that core belief, you may honor God with your mouth and serve His people with your hands, but your heart is far from Him.

God vs. Comparison

God's problem with us comparing ourselves is this: it's self-centered and unwise. Self-centered because if we're busy comparing to one another, how does God get the glory? He doesn't. Unwise because if we were knowledgeable about the Lord, we would understand that each of us have been given a boundary or a sphere of authority, as the Apostle Paul states in 2 Corinthians 10:12-16. This means that whatever God called me to do, He has given me license to do it and succeed. And as long as I stay in that sphere, it can't be a fail because God has graced me to prosper in that area. Now, if I look at someone else's sphere and try to imitate what they're doing, and want it for myself then I am bound to crash because I don't have the authority for their sphere. And that is okay because they also don't have the authority for mine. It doesn't make either of us better or worse, just different, which is what God intended. This gives a new meaning to the saying, "Stay in your lane".

The Thief of Joy

Comparison is a tool of the devil that causes division and separation among people who believe in God. Division has been his mission ever since leading Adam and Eve to sin against God in the Garden to Eden. Satan wants to tear us away from God and each other to demolish God's perfect plan of us living in communion with Him. We overcome comparison by cutting out the enemy's tools of division. We can do this by loving fiercely and staying focused. We can create unity where he seeks to create separation. We can show love and support that cries louder than our envy.

Self-awareness is required, which means knowing when you are weak or feeling tempted so you can eliminate opportunities for comparison to present itself. This looks different for us all. It's all about knowing your triggers and setting boundaries to protect your heart. For some of us, it means celebrating others outwardly whenever comparison stirs up. Sometimes it looks like unfollowing or muting people on social media— including friends, family, and influencers. It can also look like not immediately responding when someone close to you shares the exciting news that you've wanted for yourself.

Taking this route to avoid the comparison trap doesn't mean that you love these people less or that you don't care about the great things happening in their lives. It means you're trying to preserve your outlook on their life, your life, and God's will for your life. At times, the journey requires tunnel vision while you're working. There is a way to be wise with your support without being malicious. This is how I'm learning to train the voice of shame in my life. Gratefully, it has gotten quieter over time. God has given you authority in your sphere of influence. It can't be replicated and it can't be stolen.

Acknowledge Your Feelings While Honoring God

Progression doesn't come by fighting our feelings. We progress by understanding them and not allowing them to become the author of our actions. Your feelings are not the end all be all, and they are not your compass to guide how you live on this earth. Acknowledge your feelings for what they are and ask God to help you heal and push past those feelings. Seeing other people succeed in areas where we struggle and fall short touches the deepest parts of our wounds. Watching people we know or don't know achieve the things we have been longing for can reopen scars that we've worked hard to hide. Jesus Christ commands us to love our neighbor as ourselves. If you never learn how to love and respect yourself, you will always look at others through a lens of competition and not camaraderie.

The Heart of the Issue:

Comparison is the enemy's playground because he knows how easily distracting it can be to watch your desires play out in someone else's life. We are all on different journeys, and one person's acceleration does not equate to another person being slow or behind. Other people are not the standard, God is and He is the only marker we should be measured by. You have to become a gatekeeper of your heart, monitoring what enters and knowing what needs to leave. Motives are important and cannot go unchecked. You have to allow God to show you the beauty in others without feeling contention within yourself. The security will come once you know God is equally invested in developing and nurturing you.

Invocation:

God, as I take this journey, help me to discern between distractions and development. As You build a community around me, build Your character within me. Help me to remember that You are a Father who enjoys blessing His children, myself included. I have not lost, I am not behind, and I am not forgotten. In Jesus's name I pray. Amen.

"But the things
that come out of a
person's mouth come
from the heart, and
these defile them.
For out of the heart
come evil thoughts—
murder, adultery,
sexual immorality,
theft, false testimony,
slander. These are
what defile a person."

- Matthew 15:18-20

CHAPTER 3

WHEN BITTERNESS GETS THE BEST OF YOU

Are you building bitterness? Are you able to notice when bitterness is building in your heart? How do you know when it's present? It's in those moments when you think you've left everything in the past but somehow the mention of the past event triggers a reaction deep within you. Maybe it's anger, fear, or anxiety. It takes you back to how you felt at that moment and you're unable to reconcile to your present self. If you experience this often, there's probably some bitterness you are holding onto. Many of us don't believe we are capable of holding feelings of bitterness in our hearts. Most of us probably think we forgive easily as if it rolls off of us like water. But I would argue forgiveness only looks easy on the surface because it's where most of us stop forgiving. We only go skin deep in our forgiveness journey so it appears as if we have done the work and like we have healed from the hurt and dealt with the infractions against us. But below the surface, there is often much more unresolved that goes hidden from the outside, at least for a little while. Eventually, those unresolved matters have a way of bursting through the surface when we lack the self-awareness to catch them and deal with them.

Forgiveness is not pretty. It's hard and holy work, which goes against our human nature. It requires God to work through you by fully surrendering to His way through the healing journey. This will highlight the unforgiveness in your heart and give strategies on how to rip out any roots of bitterness that have formed. But if we are honest, most of us want to ignore that hard and unpretty work. We hate the discomfort it causes, we hate the mirror it holds up to our flaws and wounds, and we hate the accountability that God brings to us. Because the moment God reveals the bitterness and unforgiveness that has you bound, you are now responsible for doing the work to be fully released from it. And once we can no longer make excuses for not knowing, the only thing that's left is the truth: We don't want to forgive. It's a harsh reality but there is beauty in admitting your current truth.

Trauma has a way of making us believe our bitterness is earned and vindicated. God isn't going to punish us for admitting those feelings, He's just waiting on us to stop coming into agreement with deception. God knows you don't want to forgive the person who beat you, the person who raped you, those friends who lied about you, the family members who mocked you and betrayed you. God knows and understands the hurt that lingers in your heart and follows you daily. Once you receive the love and grace God has given you, it's time for you to be honest.

Why Is Forgiveness Required?

Forgiveness is a big deal to God. Unforgiveness is one of the simplest ways to separate ourselves from God. Praying to God requires us to forgive anyone we have issues with so that He will also forgive us. Scripture is very clear on forgiving others as God has forgiven us in Christ. It's not a suggestion, it's a command. Jesus Christ is the physical embodiment of how forgiveness is to be modeled and expressed. Christ's sole reason for coming to earth was to save humanity and restore our relationship with God. During Christ's time on earth, He experienced disappointment and serving people He knew would turn away from Him. Aside from the religious crowds that constantly sought to destroy Jesus, it was the betrayal by one of His disciples that led to His death. The very same people Jesus came to liberate were the ones who crucified Him. But Jesus knew the betrayal and disappointments were necessary.

Jesus knew what had to happen and still willingly chose to give His body as a sacrifice for those who killed Him. This is forgiveness. Forgiveness is not to be earned. You are supposed to give it freely, graciously, and without merit. It has nothing to do with the person who offended or harmed us but it has everything to do with the Forgiver (Jesus). When Jesus took on our sins and paid the penalty of death for us (Romans 6:23), He created a spiritual transaction that made us right with God and with each other. We inherited forgiveness that was undeserved, therefore we must also walk in that same forgiveness. Choosing to walk in unforgiveness or bitterness is a violation of the perfect work Jesus did on the cross. This is why God requires forgiveness. If we choose to not forgive others then that would be a contradiction of His will for us.

Unforgiveness also gives leverage to the enemy. It can evolve into a lineage of bitter and unhealthy people when not dealt with. I have some family members who have not spoken and have held grudges for longer than I have been alive, well over twenty to thirty years. That curse tried to attach itself to my heart. From a young age, I have always identified myself as a loyal person and prided myself on that for a long time. Whenever I felt someone wasn't being as loyal to me as I was to them, my cutoff game was quick! Even after I got saved, God had to deliver me from a petty mentality. You do not have to pay people back for how they treated you.

God showed me that my unwillingness to forgive limited His power in my life. He taught me that forgiveness unlocks new dimensions in life. Think about it: Forgiving frees your mind, heart, and hands. It frees your mind from consuming thoughts and memories of the person who hurt you. It frees your heart from the chains of resentment and bitterness. And it frees your hands because it releases the limitations associated with unforgiveness. You will be able to serve, live, and breathe more freely.

Forgiveness Starts With You

The first step in overcoming bitterness is admitting the truth you are in right now. Tell God the truth. Tell Him that you don't want to forgive, that you don't know how to forgive, or that you enjoyed harboring unforgiveness towards others. Whatever the case is, just be honest with Him and repent, that is the key to unlocking the forgiveness journey. Also, forgive yourself. Many of us have become bitter toward ourselves. We hold ourselves in contempt over mistakes we made in the past when we placed ourselves in compromising relationships and situations. Free your heart and forgive yourself today.

The Heart of the Issue:

Unforgiveness has a way of making a victim feel in control of what has harmed them. It's an attempt at extracting power from the place that left them feeling powerless. This is a defense mechanism that seems righteous in theory but is ineffective in practice. Choosing to not forgive will never give you the resolve you want. It will only cause your hurt to grow and fester. To receive God's best for your life, you have to release bitterness and choose forgiveness. It's not the easiest way but it is the healthiest way and eventually, your past will thank you for it.

Invocation:

Jesus, You left the perfect blueprint for forgiveness. I hope to exercise the compassion You extended, even to the most undeserving. I admit bitterness gave me a false sense of relief but now I know forgiveness brings me closer to God. Please comfort me as I release others and myself from the bondage of past hurts and mistakes. In Jesus's name I pray. Amen.

"Do not let your
hearts be troubled.
You believe in God;
believe also in me."

– John 14:1

CHAPTER 4

IS DOUBT DRIVING YOU?

I would describe myself as a naturally cautious person. I enjoy carefully counting out the risks and rewards before making decisions, big or small. I love weighing the odds before investing my time or resources into a project. That theory may seem sound and thorough, but it's a bit incomplete and unbalanced because I usually only make those slow decisions when it's time to invest in myself. For a long time, I was committed to investing in others and divesting from myself. Why? Because I doubted my value and abilities.

I thought my overly cautious nature was a way to protect myself and discern right from wrong. But there is a thin line between doubt and discernment. Let's park here. Discernment is a spiritual gift given by God that aids in our decision-making process. It helps us determine if something is in alignment with God and His will or not. Doubt is the general feeling of uncertainty, worry, or concern about the truth or reality of something. When you live in a constant state of doubt, you are conditioning your mind, body, and spirit to mobilize your life around worry and uncertainty. If all you see and think is steeped in doubt, how will you be able to accept or even notice the truth? If we're not careful, we will be easily persuaded that our disbelief is divinely inspired when it's a sign that our heart is at war with the faith our soul requires.

Delay: The Open Door to Doubt

"Delay is not denial." Believers love to throw that saying around whenever God appears to be still, quiet, or withholding His promises from us. The idea of delayment is our human justification for our lack of patience. Have you ever noticed when your doubt is heightened, it is typically occurring in a waiting season? Generally, when we perceive our waiting season as being expired by our standards, we relabel it as delay because we get tired of waiting. A great example of this is single women and marriage.

The average woman in the United States gets married by age twenty-eight. Knowing that average, a single woman in her thirties and older may perceive her marriage as being delayed. This perception can leave cracks in her heart that our enemy (the devil) can fill with doubt. This is one way delay and doubt can feed into each other. Another scenario is when many of us face doubt in our calling, we delay ourselves by walking in procrastination. There are times it will be the enemy causing delay and sometimes it's the person in the mirror. Sometimes we make our hearts sick while waiting for a promise that God didn't make in the first place. Simply put, God cannot be delayed because His timing is perfect. This is where discernment comes in because you have to be able to distinguish God's will from your own desires and the enemy's schemes. Delay creates this lie that God is moving the finish line of our lives but nothing could be farther from the truth. Anyone or anything that is trying to convince you that God is delaying you from receiving His promises needs to be cast down in the name of Jesus.

As the world grows darker, it becomes easier to operate in doubt without realizing it. Whenever we start leaning on our own strength and understanding we cross into doubtful territory. When preparation turns into self-reliance, that's another indication of doubt. The more our thinking shifts to what we need to do instead of what God can do, doubt is surely present. Doubt is normal. We experience it because of our humanity and desire to feel certain during our circumstances. A voice feeds its way into our hearts, feeding lies to our souls. Perhaps the soundtrack of defeating thoughts in your head sounds like: It didn't work last time, so why would it work out this time? I failed last time, and I'm going to fail this time. Nothing has ever succeeded for me, and it never will. It didn't work for them, so why would it work for me? If it worked out for them, it can't possibly work out for me. I don't have what it takes to succeed.

Have you ever thought or said any of these things? You are not alone in your thoughts and do not have to be stuck in your unbelief. I walked this line with doubt for a while because I struggled with my identity for so long. Whenever God called me to do something I would immediately respond in refusal. I'd say, "No, that's not for me" or "Lord, I can't do this because the money and the resources aren't here". Even as I wrote this book, I fought with doubt to release these words that you are reading. I didn't realize my denial was a door for the enemy to exploit my doubt even more. When you go into a situation with doubt, the outcome will always look cloudy because you are never satisfied with yourself. And that's an issue because we rely on ourselves to do it all when God never intended for us to do anything alone.

Is Faith the Answer to All Doubt?

Faith is often the glue that's used to fill the doubtful cracks in our hearts. And though it is a great solution, many of us still struggle to have the faith it requires to cancel our consistent doubt. Why is that? Because faith is useless when you don't have trust. You can have faith that God will make a way, but you may not trust that He will make one for you. Contrary to what we may think or have been taught, having faith does not cancel our doubt because many of us believe in a supernatural God, yet we don't trust

Him with the reins of our life due to inner doubt. When God says He wants to do something great in your life and your immediate response is how disqualified and undeserving you are, that's an indication you may not trust God to use your life as an instrument for His glory.

Doubt and trust are heart issues that must be dealt with because doubt keeps many of us stuck in stagnant seasons and dormant in our purpose. Trust is the foundation that builds strength and patience in your journey. Trust is an ingrained knowing, having confidence, and expectation of something. How do we get that confidence in God? How do we get ingrained knowing that His words and plans for us are just as true as anything else He says? Start with opening the lines of communication.

Trust is gained through relationship. It requires regularly seeking and communicating with God. Spend time learning about Him, talking with Him, and seeking ways to connect with Him. God gave us a book of references that support His nature and who He is. We operate in trust when we start to apply what we learn. But there must be an openness and willingness to not only receive the word of God but to live it. You can start by trusting Him with pieces of your life at a time, and the more vulnerable you are, the more your life will start to enhance. But just like any other relationship, commitment is required to get the fullness of the experience. So if you want the fullness of God to rule your life, you have to be willing to give Him your all. Nothing happens overnight. We have to learn to be patient in our walk with God because although He could do all things immediately, He knows that certain things require our development and maturity.

When you stay consistent in your commitment to God, you will begin to see the testament of His faithfulness in your life. And once faith is built, your confidence will be not in your abilities or gifts, but in the God who gave them to you. That's how we shrink doubt, by remembering who God is and what He's done for us. God will never miss a chance to prove His faithfulness and love toward you. Fighting doubt requires action: Focus on what God said and be obedient. How do I know? This book you are holding is a testament of what trusting God looks like. I promise the uncertainty you feel does not compare to the freedom on the other side of this doubt.

The Heart of the Issue:

Doubt is powerful and can be easily disguised as being cautious or modest. But we have to check the intentions behind our actions even when they seem right because there could be doubt present that's hindering our growth. Some people will not be willing to confront their doubt and build trust in God because they have grown comfortable living in their insecurities. But that will only breed self-resentment and envy of others. Those who are willing to treat their doubt will have renewed strength and confidence to continue walking in purpose even when facing idle seasons.

Invocation:

God, help my unbelief, not just my unbelief in You but in what You can do through me. Ingrain Your nature into my heart so that my faith can stand. When I think my life is too much and too hard to handle, remind me that You produce miracles on impossible grounds. In Jesus's name I pray. Amen.

"Do not be anxious about anything, but in every situation, by prayer and petition, with thanksgiving, present your requests to God. And the peace of God, which transcends all understanding, will guard your hearts and your minds in Christ Jesus."

– Philippians 4: 6-7

CHAPTER 5

THE ARMOR OF ANXIETY

Anxiety has become so normalized in our culture that it has desensitized our response to it. Where there is anxiety, there is a bigger issue connected to it. Anxiety itself is an alert to our body that something is off, that there is a need not being met in our current circumstances. But for many of us, instead of investigating the origin of our anxiety, we try to manage it by doing the very things that further feed our anxious tendencies.

We use our anxiety as an excuse to overwork and self-sustain when we weren't built to do either of those things. Anxiety can trigger perfectionism, overthinking, and control issues, which I believe are harmful acts of self-preservation. Wanting to protect ourselves from danger isn't a bad thing. It's natural as humans to defend and cover ourselves when we experience threats and crises. But that same self-preservation can become an idol and a slide to our downfall spiritually and naturally.

Levels of Anxiety

When I notice anxiety rising within me, it's when I've been busy planning and doing things out of my desires, and not God's will. My cycle became making a plan and expecting the Lord to bless it without even consulting Him about the decisions I made. Thankfully, God showed me that was a habit that I had to break. The truth is, breaking bad habits isn't easy, and neither is the healing that comes after it. God disrupting your plans and ideas can be one of the most humbling experiences. It can be heartbreaking to separate from people, habits, and patterns that we linked to our identity. For many of us, we believed our freedom was wrapped in those things, which is why God had to strip it away so we can learn to rely on Him only.

I have feared and resisted new transitions orchestrated by God. Truthfully, God broke my plans, but it felt like He was breaking me. The more He asked me to give something up—money, jobs, relationships, faulty mindsets—the more exposed I felt. If there's something I despise more than being unprepared, it's being exposed. And that was the very thing God wanted to show me, that my anxiety was directly tied to my need for control, protection, and hiding.

Whenever I felt uncertain and didn't know every detail of how things would work out, anxiety would harass me until I was ruminating over every possible negative outcome. And that was just the inner battle that was going on. Outwardly, I believed I was making strategic choices, but they were manipulative decisions to protect myself from people I knew loved me and had my best interests at heart. I was lying, telling people I was fine, and refusing help while withholding my true feelings and needs. Meanwhile, I was dying on the inside as I tried to figure everything out on my own. I did all of this because I was scared to let people see me struggle. I didn't want them to see me as vulnerable, nor did I want to risk being misunderstood. I had a deep-seated fear of disappointing others.

In an attempt to self-preserve, you think it will benefit you and others when in actuality it's harmful to you, which means it's dangerous for everyone connected to you. You have to assess what stimulates your anxiety and uproot the fears attached to it. Your worry is a warning. But it's not discernment because the Lord will never fill us with worry when trying to warn us. Discernment works as divine communication from God to us. It is a spiritual gift requiring a spiritual response. So if God gives us a warning, our response should be prayer, praise, and worship. This response will stop worry from building in our hearts. Worry is the natural response that causes our minds to fixate and obsess over things we have no control over. Worry is a response wrapped in flesh because it is fueled by our five physical senses: touch, taste, smell, hearing, and sight. Our natural senses are a gift from God, but the enemy can exploit them and use them to plant worry in our hearts. If we are worrying, that's a red flag that we are lacking faith and trust in God in some area of our lives. We strive to live a fully protected life, but only God can perfectly preserve His people.

Pride Before Fall

Pride is heavily attached to our desire to self-preserve. It will keep you from forging new relationships out of the desire to be "self-made". It can also keep you from deepening relationships due to anxiety of trust and vulnerability. I am familiar with this mixture of pride and anxiety and have used it as an armor in my life. Being transparent and vulnerable would invoke so much anxiety within me that I would intentionally push friends away because I didn't want them to know me. My past experiences taught me that vulnerability was dangerous because if given the chance, everyone would use it against me. This led me away from sharing my true personality and any problems I faced because I didn't want anyone to have the upper hand on me.

Many of us are reluctant to depend on others based on our traumatic experiences with people. We think we are guarding our hearts, but we aren't because that requires God's wisdom. If we were to be honest, usually when we cut people off, it has nothing to do with God and everything to do with our flesh. We don't want people to think they influence us. So if they hurt us, it's easier to say we don't need people. As a result, we close off our hearts from our next friendships and relationships. God needs to use people and problems to bless and build you. What if anxiety is keeping quality people from entering your life? What do you do when your anxiety hinders you from cultivating the best version of yourself? Improper armor may appear protective, but it will only result in your impairment.

The Heart of the Issue:

Anxiety presents itself as a friend and comfort to the damage in our hearts but allowing it to linger without addressing it will only deepen the wounds we try to hide. Do you dislike change or is it that you have some underlying control issues? Do you really not get along with most people or do you have a fear of vulnerability and abandonment? Everyone needs help. God created us to need Him and people. A self-reliant mentality and the "I can do it all alone" attitude is a choice to live an impoverished life. The armor of anxiety doesn't protect you from potential dangers. It blocks you from potential help.

Invocation:

Dear Lord, I wear anxiety like it's an accessory that I can't leave home without. It serves as a protective casing to my heart. My plans give me a sense of control and independence in life when faced with uncertainty. But I realize this armor and my plans may be hindering the bigger plan You have for me. I want to live a more trusting and fulfilling life, which requires new levels of openness for me. Surround me with people who I can be vulnerable with and who hold me accountable. Help me to find peace and confidence in You so I can become who I was created to be. In Jesus's name I pray. Amen.

"Peace I leave with you; my peace I give you. I do not give to you as the world gives. Do not let your hearts be troubled and do not be afraid."

- John 14:27

CHAPTER 6

WHEN AVOIDANCE BECOMES A LIFESTYLE

What's the difference between fear and anxiety? I define anxiety as the response to our fears. While fear is the match, anxiety is the fire. Fear is the driver while anxiety is the GPS directing each of our worried steps. Fear fuels anxiety and anxiety can make you do some crazy things. It makes you act out of character and do things you normally would not, all as a tactic of escapism. Anxiety doesn't care who you have to become and what you have to do to get away from a trigger, as long as the outcome is driving you away from the fear. Anxiety can be a good force used to push us toward our finish lines and help us stay productive and creative. But the line is drawn when our fears begin to pull us in an opposite direction toward procrastination and stagnancy. You may be familiar with the common "fight or flight" response, but there is a third response called "freeze". It is a fear response that is often neglected. Freeze is the fear response that makes us unable to move or act against a perceived threat. Anxiety will cause you to run (flight) or face your fear (fight), but fear can keep you paralyzed (freeze).

There are many variations of fear. We all experience different types and origins. Some fears are harmless because they don't affect our day-to-day lives nor hinder our progress. But I'm not addressing your fear of clowns, spiders, or dolls. I'm speaking to the fear that keeps you from pursuing your purpose. The fear that tells you to avoid, deflect and disobey God along with the assignments He's called you to do. Fear will have you hovering over a promise instead of seizing it as your own. Fear will convince you to forfeit opportunities because they look unreachable, impossible, and too great for you. It will keep you avoiding every possible blessing. How does fear become so deeply seated in our hearts? If God didn't give us a spirit of fear, why does it have such a stronghold in our lives?

Fear is birthed in areas of disappointment and uncertainty. Unknown factors put us in fear when outcomes are unclear. I walked in the fear of failure for the greater part of my life. Just the possibility of failure was enough to delay or deter my response. I was in a deep avoidance of anything that seemed out of my norm or contrary to how I saw myself. I developed this fear from a young age when I learned the pain and discomfort that came when things happened outside of what was expected. When there was a standard that I didn't meet, the judgment was always louder than the praise. So it birthed this voice that said, "What are people going to think if I do this?" and "What will people say if I get it wrong again?"

The fear of man will lead to your disobedience every time. There has to be a deep rewiring of our brains and hearts in this matter. I had to reframe how I viewed failure and success. Failure to the world looks much different than failure to the Kingdom of God.

My reverence for God and my love for Him and His people began to outweigh the fears in my heart. It took time, and it's being built every day, but you have to choose to be committed to God over people and yourself. Your fear and your obedience have to have a conversation when they conflict with one another. There will be times when God calls you to the unknown and you have to do it scared. True success is listening to God and having the faith to go after what He said regardless of what it looks like.

The Heart of the Issue:

Fear has many levels. Fear of success, fear of failure, and fear of man are common and destructive. It can be arresting and deceitful, keeping us from reaching our highest potential and discovering the fullness of who God created us to be. The origin of fear always begins with a lie that says pursuing the other side of our mountain will lead to our destruction, that the thing we fear will consume us. So instead of conquering the mountain, we stay paralyzed in place, avoiding the process and the outcome. Fear leaves no room for optimism. You have to invite hope into your fear in a way that challenges you to think, "What if I succeed?" or "What if I survive past the fear?" You deserve to dream with optimism. If you give your heart the space to be hopeful again, fear has to take a backseat.

Invocation:

Lord, I have allowed fear to narrate my life and my decisions for too long. Fear told me it would be better to settle or not try because discomfort would destroy me. Forgive me for the times I gave into fear and fled in disobedience instead of standing firm on Your Word. Give me the strength to launch even through adversity. I may do it scared, but I will never be alone. In Jesus's name I pray. Amen.

"He heals the brokenhearted and binds up their wounds."

- Psalm 147:3

CHAPTER 7

HOPE FOR THE BROKENHEARTED

As a child, I remember being consistently hopeful. It was the type of hope that was endless and life-giving. No matter what happened, I remember waking up with renewed hope. The next day always held this promise of brighter and better. There was always something to look forward to in the near future. Hope gave me an expectation that greater was not only possible but it was on the way. Do you remember that feeling?

Sometimes I wonder how hope gets so far away from us. I believe that's partially why the Lord tells us to come to Him like a child because kids are blank slates. It's not until we're older that we start wearing the residue of our deferred hopes and dreams. I could not end this book without addressing those of us who are in a season of hopelessness and dealing with broken hearts. Proverbs 13:12 says, "Hope deferred makes the heart sick, but a longing fulfilled is a tree of life." I know many of us are in that space of deferred hopes, and many of us are in a place of trying to mend our sick hearts. Hopelessness isn't easily seen or noticed. It's gradually siphoned from our hearts to where we don't realize it's gone until we are depleted. It's not your fault that the world has snatched hope from you or that people have broken your heart. Maybe you've been abused, mistreated, disappointed, and misjudged more than you can count. People have manipulated you and leached from you, and you are exhausted. Not only are you exhausted with people, but part of you feels disgruntled with God and you're in a place of wrestling with Him.

Sometimes God allows our hearts to be broken and for our hopes to appear delayed. As painful as it is, it has a purpose. God's desire is not to make your heart sick or have you bound to brokenheartedness. These are not areas meant for you to fold, but to flourish. In the moments you want to detach out of hurt and frustration, God wants to use that for your good. He wants your heart reunited with His. It's a process that comes with trials, betrayals, and refinement. If God allows your heart to be broken, He is faithful to build it back up. But next time, the rebuilt version of yourself will be better and stronger. God wants to reignite your hope in Him. He misses your childish days when you were filled with hope, blindly trusting Him. I pray that we can reach that level of hope again. Hope can be renewed and multiplied. It is the ground we need for our faith to blossom. If a hope fulfilled is a tree of life, God is turning your life into a garden.

The Heart of the Issue:

We were all built to be broken. That can be a painful truth for many of us because we wonder why God would allow us to get to the brink of hurt and hopelessness. Consider this: God knows the world and its problems are fleeting, no matter how magnified they feel and appear to us. He knows the big picture and that this earth can never satisfy our deepest hopes. That's why hope doesn't come from the world, it comes from the Creator of the world. Maybe our hope has dwindled because we look to the world and its objects as the resource of hope instead of a byproduct. Children understand this level of hope because they know since their parents are watching over them, their protection and provision is guaranteed. They know that no matter what happens, good or bad, their parents will be there as a safeguard. And this allows them to hope more freely, with an expectation of a better tomorrow. God is an awesome Father. He wants us to live in this same childlike hope with the expectation that since we have Him, we are guaranteed a better future.

Invocation:

Father, this world is riddled with pain, uncertainty and sadness. In every moment I am aware of my brokenness and imperfections, knowing that I have little control over life's issues. These problems tear at my heart and empty me of hope. Please help me to live in the hope You set aside for me in Your plans well before my birth as you said in Jeremiah 29:11. Your Word also says You are a father to the fatherless, so I know I am not a child that has been abandoned with no parental supervision. Refill my heart with hope that only comes from being attached to You. Thank You for being my safeguard. In Jesus's name I pray. Amen.

"Above all else,
guard your heart,
for everything
you do flows from it."

- Proverbs 4:23

CONCLUSION

HEART CHECK

At the beginning of the book, I mentioned this would feel like spiritual open-heart surgery. How is your heart feeling? Maybe it's a little tender from being exposed and challenged or maybe you're still evaluating some old wounds. I know it can be difficult to confront the things that have sustained our hearts for so long. But I pray you use this book as a guidepost in standing firm when the opposition tries to keep you bound. You are not what hurt you. You don't have to wear the wounds of your past as a shelter of shame. All hearts need redemption and continual reminders to stay in the right posture.

The right posture requires alignment and adjustment. Let God divinely realign you. Every surgery requires maintenance appointments and a recovery plan. When you feel your heart stirring with bad habits, don't be afraid to challenge its motives and reframe your intentions. The heart can be deceptive and wicked, which is why we must give it back to God every chance we get. Make it your habit to follow up with the Surgeon (God) regularly. No matter how far we feel from

God, He delights in redeeming our brokenness. If you have ever lived with a broken heart, you are the perfect candidate for this redemption.

A redeemed heart is not a perfect heart. It's a heart that knows of its brokenness. This redemption is for beaten, bruised, and seared hearts that are on the verge of never hoping, loving, and desiring again. God's will for us all is to stay tenderhearted and the only way to do that is to stay tethered to His heart. The closer we are to the heart of God, the easier it becomes to recover from our heart troubles. We are guaranteed to experience heartache. Thankfully, this heartache qualifies us for the ultimate recovery plan.

ACKNOWLEDGEMENTS

God, thank you for entrusting me with this book. Only You could inspire a hopeful message out of a seemingly hopeless place. As Your daughter, I am honored and forever grateful!

Writing a book is soul work. A lot of it requires you to dig into parts of yourself you never knew were present. You have good days and bad days, moments when you feel inspired and others when you question every word you've written. I am no exception to this. This is why everyone should be connected to a community of people that remind them who they are and push them to keep going. While writing this book, I was healing from my own heart issues and God forced me to lean into my surroundings like never before. And I'm glad He did because this book wouldn't be possible without Him or those around me.

Thank you to my parents, Kenneth and Laterria Simmons and to all my family members for always supporting my work, believing in me, and never missing an opportunity to show up for me.

To Antwan Lance, my life partner, you've seen the hidden tears and the triumphs. Thank you for being the gentle yet firm voice always cheering in my corner.

A special thanks to my City of Hope church family and my pastors, Bruce and Amber Robinson. Your covering, love, and leadership means the world to me.

Thank you to everyone that played any part in the construction of this book. I had a few trusted friends and purpose partners to proofread: Cleva, India, Kiera, Pamela, Tammey, Tequila, Tiffany, and Tonisha. I pray every encouraging word you all have prayed and poured into me, be multiplied back to you tenfold!

Last but not least, thank you to my book readers. You are not a faceless audience to me and I hope this book has provided you with some relief and guidance in your journey.

xoxo,
Latrice

ABOUT THE AUTHOR

Latrice Simmons is a faith-based writer and blogger. She is the creator of the Lift Her Up Society which is a community dedicated to inspiring and uplifting women from all walks of life as they pursue God and their purposes. The community began as the Lift Her Up Blog and evolved into the Lift Her Up Podcast which is available across streaming platforms including a video format on Youtube. Latrice releases a monthly newsletter called Freedom Friday that encourages readers to live in the freedom Christ has promised them. She loves being in fellowship with her local community and meeting new people. When she's not writing, she enjoys reading, going to Saturday brunch, solving puzzles, and taking a walk. Latrice currently resides in her hometown of Columbia, South Carolina.

Keep in touch with Latrice by visiting https://latriceliftherup.wordpress.com/